from SEA TO SHINING SEA

Nevada

By Dennis Brindell Fradin and Judith Bloom Fradin

CONSULTANTS

Jeffrey M. Kintop, M.A., State Archives Manager, Nevada State Library and Archives

Robert L. Hillerich, Ph.D., Professor Emeritus, Bowling Green State University;
Consultant, Pinellas County Schools, Florida

CHILDRENS PRESS®
CHICAGO

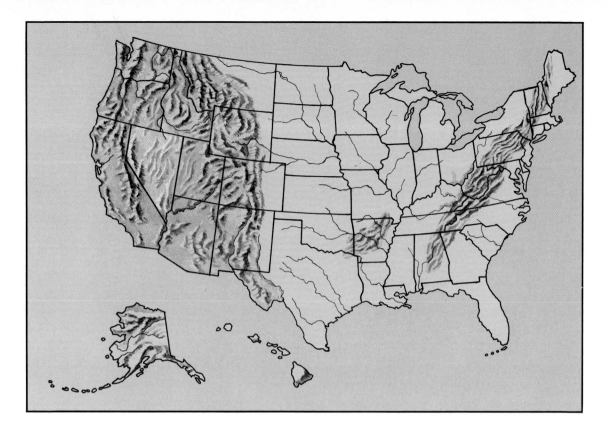

Nevada is one of the six Rocky Mountain states. The other Rocky Mountain states are Colorado, Idaho, Montana, Utah, and Wyoming.

For Davida and David Coleman, our aunt and uncle, with love

For their help, the authors thank the staff of the Nevada State Library and Archives, Carson City.

Front cover picture: Riders in the Jarbridge Wilderness; page 1: Joshua trees; back cover: Lake Tahoe

Project Editor: Joan Downing
Design Director: Karen Kohn
Photo Researcher: Jan Izzo
Typesetting: Graphic Connections, Inc.
Engraving: Liberty Photoengraving

Library of Congress Cataloging-in-Publication Data

Fradin, Dennis B.
  Nevada / by Dennis Brindell Fradin & Judith Bloom Fradin.
    p.   cm. — (From sea to shining sea)
  Includes index.
  ISBN 0-516-03828-1
  1. Nevada—Juvenile literature. [1. Nevada.] I. Fradin, Judith Bloom. II. Title. III. Series: Fradin, Dennis B. From sea to shining sea.
F841.3.F69   1995   95-13419
979.3—dc20   CIP
                                                             AC

Table of Contents

Dancers at the Stewart Powwow in Carson City

INTRODUCING THE SILVER STATE

Nevada is in the southwestern United States. Huge deserts give the state a special beauty. The snowcapped peaks of the Sierra Nevada gave the state its name. *Nevada* is a Spanish word for "snowfall."

For hundreds of years, American Indians had Nevada to themselves. Then, in 1859, miners found gold and silver in Nevada. Thousands of people came to live and work there. In 1864, during the Civil War, Nevada became a state. That's why one of Nevada's nicknames is the "Battle Born State."

The words Battle Born *are on the Nevada state flag.*

Today, Nevada leads the country in mining silver and gold. The "Silver State" is Nevada's main nickname. Gambling is legal throughout the state. Casinos in Nevada's largest cities draw millions of visitors each year.

Much more is special about the Silver State. In what state did the first woman run for the United States Senate? Where were the Indian holy man Wovoka and tennis star Andre Agassi born? Which state has the tallest concrete dam and the largest reservoir? Which state has been growing the fastest? The answer to these questions is: Nevada!

A picture map
of Nevada

Overleaf: The
Granite Range

CASINO

SALOON

LUCKY

CASINO

5

Snowcapped Mountains, Sandy Deserts

SNOWCAPPED MOUNTAINS, SANDY DESERTS

Nevada is a Rocky Mountain State. It covers 110,540 square miles in that part of the country. Five states border Nevada. Oregon and Idaho are to the north. Utah and Arizona are to the east. California is to the south and west.

Over three-fourths of Nevada is desert. The Great Basin Desert covers much of the state. The Mojave Desert is in southeastern Nevada. More than 150 mountains rise up over the deserts. The Sierra Nevada is among the state's many mountain

Left: Elephant Rock Arch, Valley of Fire State Park
Right: The Ruby Mountains

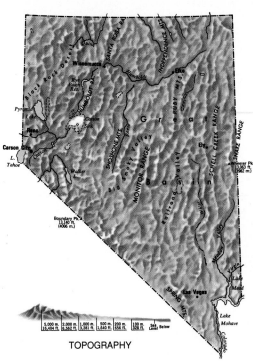

TOPOGRAPHY

ranges. At 13,140 feet, Boundary Peak is the state's tallest mountain. Only eight states have a higher mountain. Nevada's average height is 5,500 feet. Only four states are higher than that.

Left: Red Rock Canyon

Nevada has many huge rock formations. In places, there are deep gashes in the land. They are called canyons. Steep hills called buttes rise sharply above Nevada. The Silver State also has flat-topped mountains. They are called mesas.

CLIMATE

Nevada is the driest of the fifty states. Deserts receive under 10 inches of precipitation a year.

9

The Carson River, near Dayton

Four of every five days are sunny in Nevada.

Nevada gets only 9 inches of rain and melted snow a year. Whirlwinds of sand and dust sometimes form over Nevada's deserts. These are called "dust devils."

Nevada summers are hot. July days can top 105 degrees Fahrenheit in southern Nevada. But nighttime summer temperatures can drop to 50 degrees Fahrenheit. That's because of Nevada's dry air. Yet, Nevada winters can get quite cold. Temperatures below 20 degrees Fahrenheit are not unusual in the north.

Nevada's lowest lands receive little snow. But some mountains get over 20 feet of snow a year. Sometimes, Nevada has thick winter fogs with frost crystals. They are called *pogonips.* This is a Shoshone word for "clouds."

WATER, PLANTS, AND ANIMALS

Only 1/150 of Nevada is covered by water. Few states have a lower rate of water to land. The Humboldt is the state's longest river. It winds for 300 miles across northern Nevada. The Carson and Truckee are two other major rivers in Nevada. The Colorado River flows along part of the border with Arizona.

Nevada and California share Lake Tahoe. This is North America's largest mountain lake. Lake Tahoe

Stella Lake, Great Basin National Park

covers 192 square miles. Pyramid Lake is the largest natural lake completely within Nevada. It occupies 188 square miles. But Nevada's biggest lake of all is man-made. In fact, Lake Mead is the largest artificial lake in the country. This 250-square-mile lake is mostly in Nevada. Part of it lies in Arizona. Hoover Dam on the Colorado River formed Lake Mead.

Many kinds of trees grow in Nevada's mountains. The single-leaf piñon is one of Nevada's two state trees. The wood of this small pine burns with a sweet aroma. The bristlecone pine is Nevada's other state tree. Bristlecone pines live longer than any other tree. Joshua trees, a kind of yucca, grow in Nevada's deserts.

Bristlecone pines can live more than 5,000 years.

An ocotillo plant

Twenty-eight different kinds of cactus plants grow in Nevada. Sagebrush covers one-fifth of the state. This desert shrub is the state flower. Nevada is sometimes called the "Sagebrush State." The creosote bush is another desert shrub in Nevada. When it blooms, parts of the desert become oceans of yellow. The ocotillo plant has flame-colored flowers. They look like candles. The ocotillo can grow 20 feet high.

The desert bighorn sheep is Nevada's state animal. This wild sheep has very large horns. Nevada is

home to about **30,000** mustangs. No other state has more of these wild horses. Wild burros also roam about Nevada. So do pronghorns and mule deer. The desert tortoise is Nevada's state reptile. It can weigh ten pounds and live seventy-five years. The mountain bluebird is Nevada's state bird. Many bald eagles, golden eagles, hawks, and falcons fly about the state. Pelicans and osprey fish in Nevada's waters. Twenty-six kinds of lizards live in Nevada. The banded Gila monster is the only poisonous kind. Chuckwallas and zebratails are harmless lizards. Poisonous rattlesnakes also live in Nevada. Trout, bass, and catfish swim in Nevada waters. The Lahontan cutthroat trout is the state fish.

Wild burros

Burros are also called donkeys. Pronghorns are often called antelopes.

FROM ANCIENT TIMES UNTIL TODAY

Millions of years ago, shallow seas covered Nevada. Giant sea reptiles called ichthyosaurs swam about. Today, the ichthyosaur is the state fossil. Saber-toothed tigers and camels also lived in Nevada.

AMERICAN INDIANS

The first people reached Nevada about 13,000 years ago. Early Nevadans lived in caves and rock shelters. They hunted with spears. These early people tracked bisons and mammoths. About 2,300 years ago, people called Basket Makers lived in Nevada. These Indians lived in pit houses. They made baskets from sagebrush and other plants.

Over time, some early Indians learned to farm. The Anasazi were a farming people. Their culture reached its peak in Nevada around the year 900. The Anasazi grew corn and beans. They irrigated their fields. They put up buildings made of dried mud bricks. Some buildings had 100 rooms. One Anasazi village is called Pueblo Grande de Nevada. It's also known as the Lost City. Part of Pueblo

Petroglyphs (rock art) in Valley of Fire State Park

Opposite: The Genoa Courthouse Museum

15

Indian dancers in the Lost City

Grande now lies beneath Lake Mead. Around the year 1150, the Anasazi disappeared from Nevada.

The Paiute, Washo, and Shoshone then moved into Nevada. In winter, these Indians lived in wicki-ups. These were domed huts made of bark and brush. In summer, they rested under a roof held up by four poles. Nevada's Indians hunted rabbits and pronghorns with bows and arrows. They caught fish, ducks, and geese with nets. The Indians ground piñon nuts into flour. From it, they made

16

biscuits and cakes. They brewed sagebrush tea. Juniper bark was used for clothing and rope.

Each tribe divided into separate groups. At times, a tribe's groups gathered together. They then performed old dances. They held races and archery contests. Some tribe members told their people's old stories.

Today's Indians gather at powwows just as their ancestors did.

EARLY EXPLORERS, FUR TRADERS, AND SETTLERS

In the 1500s, Spain took over Mexico. Its rule also covered much of the present-day southwestern United States. This included Nevada. Not until 1776, however, did any Spaniards enter Nevada. In that year, Father Francisco Garcés is believed to have entered Nevada. He stopped at present-day Las Vegas. Garcés wrote about a place he called *Las Vegas.* That Spanish term means "the meadows" in English.

In 1821, Mexico broke free of Spain. Mexico also claimed Spain's lands in the southwest, including Nevada. However, Mexico did not explore or settle Nevada.

By 1732, England ruled thirteen colonies along the Atlantic Ocean. In 1776, the colonies declared their independence. They became the United States

The Kit Carson statue on the capitol grounds

An interior view of the Genoa Courthouse Museum

of America. The young country sent explorers west in the 1800s. Americans didn't reach Nevada until 1826. Fur trader and explorer Jedediah Smith came to Nevada in that year. John C. Frémont was another American. He explored Nevada in 1843. The well-known frontiersman Kit Carson guided him. Nevada's Carson River and Carson City were named for Kit.

By the 1840s, the United States wanted Mexico's lands in the Southwest. The United States and Mexico went to war in 1846. The United States won the Mexican War in 1848 and took over Nevada and other southwestern lands.

Gold was found in California in 1848. Thousands of gold seekers passed through Nevada on their way to California. A few stopped in Nevada to mine or farm. Members of the Mormon religious group also came to Nevada. In 1851, they built a trading post near Lake Tahoe. California-bound gold hunters bought supplies at this outpost. It was called Mormon Station. Nevada's first town, Genoa, grew up at Mormon Station. In 1855, the Mormons also built a settlement at present-day Las Vegas. A few years later they left. Carson City was founded in 1858. Still, Nevada had only about 1,000 settlers by early 1859.

GOLD, SILVER, AND STATEHOOD

In February and June 1859, Nevada miners made rich gold strikes. With further digging, they found silver, too. The deposit was named for miner Henry Comstock. The Comstock Lode was one of the world's richest silver deposits. It also contained plenty of gold. Miners flocked to the Comstock Lode. A few gained great wealth.

Virginia City was begun near the Comstock Lode in 1859. This town was a rough place. Saloons had names like the "Bucket of Blood." Gamblers tried to win the miners' silver and gold. Outlaws robbed stagecoaches on the roads near town.

This picture of an overland stagecoach at Carson City was taken in the 1860s.

By 1861, Virginia City had 20,000 people. That year, the United States government made Nevada a territory. Also in that year, the Civil War (1861-1865) began. The southern slave states fought against the northern free states.

President Abraham Lincoln wanted Nevada to become a state for two reasons. First, most Nevadans opposed slavery. Statehood for Nevada would mean more votes in Congress for the abolition of slavery. Second, the new state would give Lincoln three more Republican electoral votes in the next presidential election. Nevada became the thirty-sixth state on October 31, 1864. About 1,100 Nevadans fought for the Union. The Union victory in 1865 freed the southern slaves.

New towns were founded in the young state. Eureka began in 1864. It was at the site of a silver and lead discovery. Reno began in 1868 as a railroad town. Ely started in 1868 as a gold-mining camp. By 1870, Nevada had about 43,000 people.

A mint is a place where coins are made.

Nevada mined so much gold and silver that the United States government opened a mint there. The Carson City mint ran from 1870 to 1893. Its coins were marked "CC." By 1880, though, much of the Comstock Lode's riches had been mined. Many Nevadans turned to cattle ranching as mining fell

off. Cowboys cared for the cattle on the ranches. Sheep raising also became important.

An 1875 picture of the Carson City mint

NEW TOWNS, IRRIGATION, WORLD WARS, AND DEPRESSION

In 1900, Jim Butler made a big silver discovery. Nearby, he founded the silver-mining town of Tonopah. In 1902, Butler grubstaked two other miners. They found gold. The town of Goldfield was built near their discovery. In 1905, the town of Las Vegas was founded. At first, it was a railroad town. Today, Las Vegas is one of the youngest major cities in the United States.

Grubstaking *means providing miners with food and supplies in return for a share of what they find.*

21

Meanwhile, Nevada farmers had trouble. They had to get water to their dry lands. Nevadan Francis Newlands helped with this problem. Newlands served in the United States House of Representatives (1893-1903) and the Senate (1903-1917). He sponsored the 1902 Newlands Reclamation Act. It set aside United States government money for irrigation. Nevada began the country's first federal irrigation project. The Newlands Irrigation Project was completed in 1907. Nevada's western desert then had water. Crops grew where once there had been sand.

Melons growing in irrigated soil, 1910

In 1917, the United States entered World War I (1914-1918). About 5,500 Nevadans went to war. Nevada's beef cattle and sheep helped feed the soldiers. Its horses served on the field of battle. Then, the Great Depression (1929-1939) hit the country. Banks, farms, mines, and factories failed. But Nevada found new ways to bring money into the state. In 1931, Nevada legalized gambling. This law turned Las Vegas and Reno into major entertainment centers. Casinos and hotels went up in both cities. No other state allowed wide-open gambling. Also in 1931, Nevada made it easy for couples to get divorced. Reno became known as the divorce capital of the world.

In 1941, the United States entered World War II (1939-1945). About 20,000 Nevadans served. Nellis Air Force Base was built near Las Vegas. A navy air base was built at Fallon. Metals from Nevada also helped win the war.

Nevada legalized gambling in 1931.

RECENT CHALLENGES AND SUCCESSES

During the war, the United States began making nuclear weapons. Nuclear testing continued after the war. The Nevada Test Site was built northwest of Las Vegas. In 1951, atomic bomb tests were first held there. More tests followed. Nuclear tests still take place there. Since 1963, though, they have been done underground.

A 1967 state law allowed large businesses to own casinos. Airplane-maker Howard Hughes bought many Las Vegas casinos. Large companies built hotels and casinos in Las Vegas and Reno. Both cities grew rapidly. Between 1970 and 1994, the population of Las Vegas tripled. Reno's population doubled.

Las Vegas now suffers from big-city troubles. Crime has risen. Race relations in the city are poor. Schools can't be built quickly enough for all the new students. Many cars are causing air pollution.

The state's population as a whole has also grown. In 1950, Nevada had 160,000 people. That was the smallest population of all the states. Since then, many people have moved to Nevada. They work in its mining, gambling, and tourist industries. Large numbers of retired people have settled there, too. By 1994, Nevada had 1.5 million people. That's nearly ten times its 1950 figure. Now, Nevada is the fastest-growing state.

Since the 1970s, Nevadans have done microscopic gold mining. Small amounts of gold are obtained from tons of rock. This fueled a northeast-

ern Nevada mining boom. The town of Elko has seen great growth.

Jet-skiing on Lake Tahoe

The Silver State faces problems, however. In places, mining and nuclear tests have damaged the land and water. Water is still an important matter in Nevada. Microscopic gold mining, hotels, and homeowners need huge amounts of water. Few states use more water per person than Nevada. A drought between 1988 and 1992 made Nevada's water problems worse.

Nevadans have overcome problems before. They built farms in places that were once too dry for farming. They created cities in the desert. Now, Nevadans must make plans to keep the Silver State's future bright.

Overleaf: A Virginia City banjo player

Nevadans and Their Work

Nevadans and Their Work

In the 1990 census, Nevada had about 1.2 million people. Four years later, there were 1.5 million Nevadans. Nevada is the fastest-growing state. Yet it is one of the least-crowded states. There are just 11 people per square mile there.

Of every 100 Nevadans, 84 are white. Most of their backgrounds are German, English, or Irish. About 150,000 Hispanic-Americans live in Nevada. More than half of their families came from Mexico. About 100,000 Nevadans are black Americans. Another 50,000 are Asian Americans. Many Asian Americans are from the Philippines or China. Nevada is home to 25,000 American Indians. The Paiute and Shoshone are the largest tribes.

Though most Nevadans are white, many Hispanic-Americans, black Americans, Asian Americans, and American Indians also live in the state.

Nevadans at Work

About 750,000 Nevadans have jobs. Nearly half of them provide services. Nevada has the largest rate of service workers of any state. Many of them work in Nevada's giant tourist business. More than 38 million people visit Nevada each year. That's twenty-five times as many people as live there! Some visitors

try their luck at the state's gambling tables. Thousands of Nevadans work in hotels and casinos. Doctors, nurses, and lawyers are other Nevada service workers.

Selling goods is Nevada's second-leading kind of work. Nearly 150,000 people do this. Many of them work in restaurants and grocery stores. Nearly 100,000 Nevadans work for the government. The United States government owns about 80 percent of Nevada's land. Many Nevadans work at Nellis Air Force base and the Nevada Test Site.

About 50,000 Nevadans build new homes and offices in the state. Nevada has the country's highest

Skiing above Lake Tahoe

A cattle drive in the high desert near Smith

rate of construction workers. About 30,000 Nevadans make goods. Computers and electrical equipment are the leading products. Foods packaged in Nevada include meat, candy, and potato chips.

Nevada has about 13,000 mine workers. Only twelve states have more. Nevada leads the states at mining gold and silver. About 350,000 pounds of gold a year are mined. About 1.4 million pounds of silver a year come from Nevada. Oil, sand and gravel, and clay are other mining products.

Nevada has 2,400 farms and ranches. Beef cattle and sheep are Nevada's major farm products. Dairy cows and hogs are important, too. Hay, grapes, and onions are major crops grown in the state.

Overleaf: The Reno skyline at sunset

A Tour of the Silver State

A Tour of the Silver State

Nevada's biggest cities are lively and exciting. The state's ghost towns are fun to explore. Many visitors enjoy Nevada's mountain lakes and hiking trails.

Las Vegas

Las Vegas is a good place to start a Nevada tour. It's the state's biggest city. This southeastern Nevada town is surrounded by desert. Las Vegas is sometimes called a city of lights. At night, its lights can be seen miles away in the desert.

Las Vegas's gambling and nightlife are for adults. The city also has plenty of places for children. The Guinness World of Records Museum features exhibits on many world record holders. The museum's World of Las Vegas spotlights the city's world records. For example, eight of the world's ten largest hotels are there.

The Lied Discovery Children's Museum is there, too. It is one of the country's largest children's museums. At the museum, young people can enter a model tornado. They can learn about weath-

er and echoes. Everyday Living is another museum highlight. It has a bank, a grocery store, and a post office. There, children learn about savings accounts, writing checks, and other daily matters.

The Las Vegas Natural History Museum has giant dinosaur models. These dinosaurs have moving parts that visitors can control. Young visitors can touch fossils that are millions of years old. The Nevada State Museum is also in Las Vegas. It brings southern Nevada history to life. Other displays tell about plant and animal life in the desert. The bat cave is popular with children.

Nevada's largest college is in Las Vegas. The University of Nevada at Las Vegas (UNLV) has

Las Vegas

The UNLV Health Science Building

33

Claes Oldenburg's Flashlight *sculpture at UNLV*

Hoover Dam (below) is about seventy stories high and about one-fourth of a mile long.

about 20,000 students. A famous Claes Oldenburg sculpture called *The Flashlight* stands there. The school's Barrick Museum has live desert tortoises and chuckwallas. The UNLV Runnin' Rebels were the 1990 national basketball champions.

The National Finals Rodeo takes place in Las Vegas each December. This is the largest rodeo in the country. It offers $3 million in prizes.

OTHER SOUTHERN NEVADA HIGHLIGHTS

Hoover Dam is southeast of Las Vegas at the Arizona border. Over five years, nearly 6,000 people

built the 726-foot-tall dam. It is the country's tallest concrete dam. Hoover Dam provides water and electricity for Nevada. Parts of Arizona and California also enjoy its benefits. Visitors can go inside the dam. After visiting the dam, many people enjoy a swim in Lake Mead. This lake was formed by Hoover Dam.

The Hoover Dam Museum is in nearby Boulder City. It's a good place to learn more about the dam. Boulder City was built to house the dam's workers. Today, the town has many art galleries.

Henderson is west of Hoover Dam. It was begun in the 1940s. Today, Henderson is Nevada's

A boat marina on Lake Mead

A Hoover Dam tour

Left: The Bottle House
Right: Lake Tahoe

third-largest city. It's the state's industrial center. The Clark County Heritage Museum is in Henderson. It traces 12,000 years of Nevada history. A ghost town and old homes from around the state were moved there. Early farming and mining machinery can be seen there, too. The museum also has a 100-year-old newspaper print shop.

The Ethel M Chocolate Factory is a sweet Henderson spot. Visitors can see how chocolates are made. The Kidd Marshmallow Factory also offers tours. This Henderson company makes a million pounds of marshmallows a year.

Rhyolite is northwest of Las Vegas. It's one of Nevada's many ghost towns. In the early 1900s,

Rhyolite was a mining town. When the gold and silver ran out, the miners left. Most of the town's buildings fell apart. Many were made of mud-dried bricks. Rhyolite's Bottle House still stands, though. Miners built it with about 20,000 bottles.

Goldfield is another old mining town. It's north of Rhyolite. In 1920, Goldfield was Nevada's biggest city. The Goldfield Hotel is still standing. It was once Nevada's fanciest hotel. Tonopah is north of Goldfield. It was a big silver-mining town. Today, visitors tour the Mizpah Hotel. Tonopah's Central Nevada Museum tells about mining. Each May, Tonopah holds Jim Butler Days. Butler was Tonopah's founder. The festival includes street dancing and arm wrestling.

THE LAKE TAHOE REGION

Lake Tahoe lies at the elbow-shaped bend of the Nevada-California border. Tahoe, as the area is known, is a vacationland. In the winter, people ski there. During warmer months, they sail, water-ski, and windsurf. A boat tour is a good way to see Lake Tahoe.

Many other Nevada towns lie near Lake Tahoe. One is Genoa. It's Nevada's oldest town. Carson

City is to the north. This town has been Nevada's capital since 1861. The Nevada State Capitol was completed in 1871. The governor's office is there today. But since 1971, Nevada's legislature has met in the State Legislative Building.

The Nevada State Museum is in the old Carson City mint. The mint's old coin-making machine is there. So is one each of every coin minted at Carson City. Visitors also enjoy the museum's replica of an underground silver mine.

The Bowers Mansion is north of Carson City. Lemuel and Eilley Bowers had Comstock Lode claims. They struck it rich. In 1864, they built a

The Nevada State Museum has one branch in Las Vegas and the other in Carson City.

The Nevada State Capitol

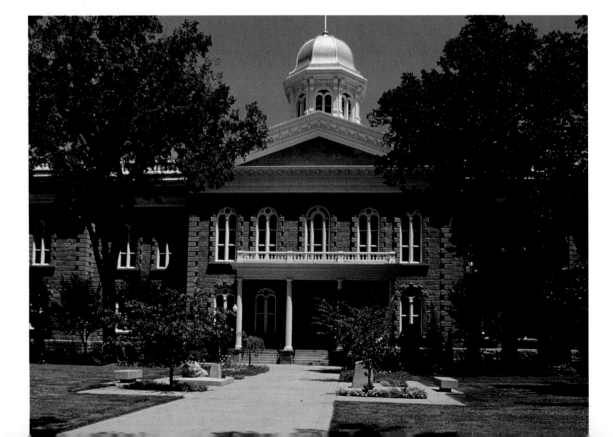

mansion and filled it with European treasures. In 1868, Lemuel died. Eilley lost her fortune and her home. Today, the sixteen-room Bowers Mansion has been restored. It looks much as it did when the Bowerses lived there.

At the end of October, Carson City celebrates Nevada Day. That's when Nevada became a state in 1864. There are parades, dances, and special exhibits.

Virginia City is north of Carson City. In the 1870s, Virginia City had 20,000 people. It was one of the world's richest mining towns. The city was known as "Queen of the Comstock Lode." Today, visitors can tour Virginia City's many old buildings.

Only about 200 people live in Virginia City (above) now. But it is not a ghost town.

The Castle is one of them. It is the grandest of Nevada's mining-era homes. The Way It Was Museum shows Virginia City during the 1860s and 1870s. The Virginia & Truckee Railroad offers tours of the Comstock Lode area. The line uses old steam locomotives. Each September, the International Camel Races are held in Virginia City. At one time, camels were used to carry supplies to miners.

Reno is north of Virginia City. This town was begun in 1868. It was named for Union Civil War general Jesse Reno. The "Biggest Little City in the World" is Reno's nickname. Today, Reno is Nevada's second-biggest city.

A view of Reno

The University of Nevada was moved from Elko to Reno in 1886. Fleischmann Planetarium is at the university. Images of the stars and planets are shown in its Star Theater. On some evenings, visitors can look through the planetarium's telescope. Reno is also home to the Nevada Historical Society Museum. Baskets woven by Dat So La Lee are among its treasures. She was a famous Washo Indian basket maker. Also at the museum, children can work a model of a stamp mill. This device was used to crush silver, gold, and other ores.

A University of Nevada-Washington State football game

The Nevada Museum of Art is also in Reno. It's Nevada's largest art museum. Works from around the world are displayed there. The National Automobile Museum is another stop for Reno visitors. This museum has 200 historic cars. A 1936 silver Mercedes-Benz is the most valuable one. This car is worth $3 million. The museum's oldest car is an 1890 Philion. It was one of the first cars made in the United States.

OTHER CENTRAL NEVADA HIGHLIGHTS

Pyramid Lake is north of Reno. It has been called the world's loveliest desert lake. Pyramid Lake is also one of the largest freshwater lakes in the West.

41

Just 77 feet shorter than Boundary Peak, Wheeler Peak (above) is Nevada's second-highest mountain.

Rock islands in Pyramid Lake

Thousands of years ago, it was part of Lake Lahontan. This ancient lake covered one-tenth of Nevada. An ancient kind of fish is the cui-ui. Today, it is found only in Pyramid Lake. The cui-ui can live forty years. Pyramid Lake's Anaho Island is a breeding ground for American white pelicans.

Stillwater National Wildlife Refuge is southeast of Pyramid Lake. Many kinds of birds gather in this wetlands area. They include ducks, swans, and ibises. Ibises have long necks and legs.

Farther southeast is Berlin-Ichthyosaur State Park. Berlin was once a gold-mining town. Today, it is one of Nevada's best-preserved ghost towns.

Remains of about forty ichthyosaurs have been found in the park. These huge sea creatures were 50 feet long. They weighed up to 120,000 pounds. Their eyes alone were a foot across. Today, visitors to the park can see ichthyosaur skeletons.

The fossil remains of an ichthyosaur at Berlin-Ichthyosaur State Park

Great Basin National Park is close to Nevada's border with Utah. This is Nevada's only national park. It has tall mountains and a huge forest. Trails lead to the top of Wheeler Peak, which is 13,063 feet above sea level. The park's forest has bristlecone pines. Some of these trees are more than 5,000 years old. Lexington Arch and Lehman Caves are other interesting sights. The arch is six stories tall. It is one of the country's largest limestone arches. The caves have many strange formations. They look like scenes from a haunted house. Visitors can hike into some of the park's canyons. They might see mountain lions, bobcats, mule deer, and golden eagles.

NORTHERN NEVADA

Northern Nevada has few people. For example, only 1,800 people live in Eureka County. Las Vegas gains that many people each month! Much of northern Nevada belongs to the federal government. Humboldt National Forest is north of Great Basin

Lehman Cave

National Park. Many national wildlife refuges and Indian reservations are also in northern Nevada.

Elko is northern Nevada's largest city. The Northeastern Nevada Museum is in this city. A Pony Express cabin from 1860 is at the museum. Riders stopped at the cabin to change horses. These riders carried mail between Missouri and California. The museum also has a display on microscopic gold mining. Three of the country's five largest gold mines are within 30 miles of Elko.

Nevada's Basque history is also told at the museum. The Basques came from the Pyrenees Mountains between France and Spain. Each July, Elko hosts the National Basque Festival. Basque games, dancing, and foods are enjoyed by all. There is also a contest for doing the *irrintzi*—the Basque yell.

The Ruby Mountains are near Elko. These snow-covered peaks are known for their rugged beauty. People ride horses in the Rubies. Skiers go by helicopter up into the mountains. Then they ski down the slopes.

Northern Nevada is also known for its cattle ranches. This part of the state is known as "Cowboy Country." Winnemucca is in north-central Nevada. The Buckaroo Hall of Fame is there. Visitors can see

Buckaroo is another name for a cowboy.

44

ropes, saddles, and guns used by old-time bucka-
roos.

The Sheldon National Wildlife Refuge is near
Nevada's northwest corner. It's a good place to end
a Nevada tour. The refuge covers 900 square miles.
It is nearly as big as the state of Rhode Island. Up to
2,500 pronghorns live in the refuge. Keen eyesight
protects these 120-pound animals from coyotes and
people. Pronghorns can also outrun every other animal in North America. They can go from 0 to 60
miles per hour in a few seconds. Wild horses and
wild burros roam the refuge, too.

*Skiers take helicopter
rides up into the
Ruby Mountains and
then ski down the
slopes.*

*Overleaf: Senator Paul
Laxalt*

45

A Gallery
of Famous
Nevadans

A GALLERY OF FAMOUS NEVADANS

Nevada has produced many great people. They include teachers, authors, tennis stars, and Indian leaders. **Winnemucca** (1799?-1882) was a Paiute chief. He tried to keep peace between the Indians and white settlers. The town of Winnemucca was named for him. **Sarah Winnemucca Hopkins** (1844?-1891) was his daughter. When Hopkins was a young woman, white people took Paiute lands. Later, she fought for her people's rights. Hopkins wrote *Life Among the Paiutes* (1883). It tells of the government's broken promises. Hopkins also taught at a school for Paiute children near Lovelock.

Wovoka (1858?-1932) was born near Nevada's Walker Lake. He became a well-known Paiute holy man. Wovoka began a new religion. It was called the Ghost Dance. This new belief promised a better future for the Indians. Wovoka said that the white people would go away. Indians would again have the land to themselves. Members of many tribes adopted Wovoka's Ghost Dance religion.

Hannah Clapp (1824-1908) was born in New York State. She moved to Carson City in 1860.

Sarah Winnemucca (above) was also called Thoc-me-tony ("Shell Flower").

47

Anne Martin

Clapp became a pioneer in education. In 1861, she began Miss Clapp's School. The school admitted both young women and young men. It was one of the West's first schools to do that. In 1877, Clapp opened Nevada's first kindergarten. Later, she moved to Reno. For many years, she was the University of Nevada's librarian.

Anne Martin (1875-1951) was born in Empire City. She later became a University of Nevada history professor. Martin led the fight for Nevada women's voting rights. Nevada women won the vote in 1914. In 1918, Martin ran for the U.S. Senate. She was the first woman in the country to do that. Martin lost, as she did again in 1920. But her work paved the way for other women to win office later.

Maude Frazier (1881-1963) was born in Wisconsin. She began teaching in Nevada in 1906. Later, Frazier became southern Nevada's school supervisor. Her district included seventy-five schools. Frazier visited them by crossing the desert in her little car. She then served in the state legislature (1951-1961). Frazier was largely responsible for founding UNLV. At eighty-one, she became Nevada's first female lieutenant governor.

Frankie Sue Del Papa was born in Hawthorne in 1949. She grew up in Tonopah. Del Papa became a lawyer. In 1987, she took office as Nevada's first female secretary of state. She was elected Nevada's first woman attorney general in 1990. Del Papa has worked on behalf of Nevada's children and senior citizens.

Paul Laxalt was born in Reno in 1922. His Basque father herded sheep in the mountains. His mother ran a Carson City restaurant and hotel. Laxalt became Nevada's governor (1967-1971). Later, he served Nevada in the U.S. Senate (1975-1987). **Robert Laxalt** (born 1923) is Paul's brother. Robert writes books about Nevada. *Sweet Promised Land* tells about his father's life as a sheepherder.

Emma Wixom sang for Austin miners when she was only five.

Two other authors also set much of their work in Nevada. **Walter Van Tilburg Clark** (1909-1971) was born in Maine. He grew up in Nevada and attended the University of Nevada. For a time, he was a high-school teacher and basketball coach. His best-known work is *The Ox-Bow Incident.* It was made into a powerful movie. **Carol Davis Luce** was born in 1943 in Indiana. She moved to Sparks as an adult. Her thrillers include *Night Stalker* and *Night Passage.* She's called the novelist who "leaves readers screaming for more."

Waddie Mitchell was born in Elko in 1950. His family's ranch had no electricity. That meant he couldn't watch television. Instead, Mitchell and the ranch hands told stories and recited cowboy poems. Mitchell became a cowboy and a poet. His poems are about cattle, ponies, and the open range. Mitchell helped start the Cowboy Poetry Gathering. It's held in Elko each January.

Emma Wixom (1859-1940) was born in California. Her family moved to Austin, Nevada, when she was five. At that young age, Emma sang for local miners. She grew up to become an opera star. She changed her name to Emma Nevada. Emma made a childhood dream come true. She sang for England's Queen Victoria.

Edna Purviance (1896-1958) was born in Paradise Valley. She grew up in Lovelock. After high school, Purviance moved to California. There, she met film comedian Charlie Chaplin. Purviance became Chaplin's leading lady. They made more than 30 films together. *The Kid* and *The Pilgrim* are two of them.

Theresa Smokey Jackson (born 1916) and **JoAnn Smokey Martinez** (born 1921) are sisters. They were born in Minden. Both are well-known Washo weavers. Their mother and grandmother taught them to weave willow baskets and cradle-

Left: When Emma Wixom grew up and became an opera star, she changed her name to Emma Nevada. Right: Edna Purviance

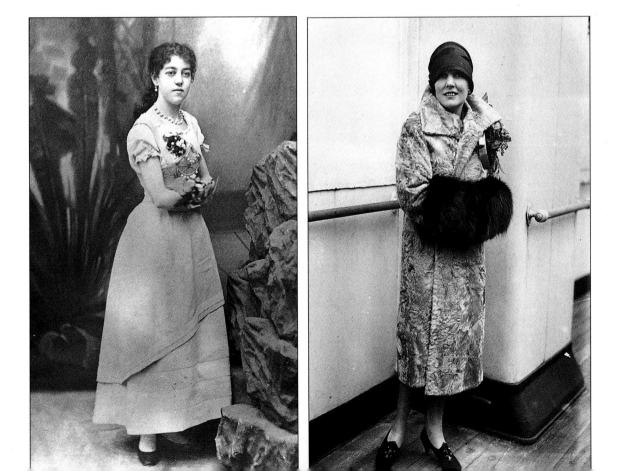

Cradleboards are used to carry babies.

Jack Kramer

boards. Theresa and JoAnn are now passing their craft on to young people. They also teach the Washo language to children on their reservation.

Two tennis stars were Las Vegas natives. **Jack Kramer** was born there in 1921. In 1946 and 1947, he won the U.S. Open Championship. Kramer was one of the best players ever. He even had a tennis racket named for him. **Andre Agassi** was born in Las Vegas in 1970. He played tennis with adults by the age of four. Agassi won the U.S. Open Championship in 1994.

Patty Sheehan was born in Vermont in 1956. When she was eleven, her family moved to Nevada. Sheehan became a great golfer. She has won many golf titles. They include the 1992 and 1994 U.S. Women's Open Golf Championships.

Greg LeMond was born in California in 1961. His family moved to Nevada when he was eight. LeMond rode his bike between Carson City and Reno to attend junior high. This is 60 miles round-trip! LeMond grew up to be a world-famous bicycle racer. In 1986, LeMond won the 2,474-mile Tour de France. He was the first American to do this. Soon after, LeMond was shot in a hunting accident. He nearly died. But in 1989 and 1990, he again won the Tour de France.

Greg Maddux was born in Texas in 1966. He grew up in Las Vegas. There, he was twice an all-state pitcher in high school. Maddux became a major-league star. He won the 1992, 1993, and 1994 Cy Young Awards. No other player has won this pitching award in three straight years.

Greg LeMond (front) won the 1989 Tour de France (above). It is the world's most famous bicycle race.

The birthplace of Jack Kramer, Edna Purviance, Wovoka, and Sarah Winnemucca Hopkins . . .

Home, too, of Greg LeMond, Greg Maddux, Maude Frazier, and Emma Nevada . . .

Site of Great Basin National Park, Hoover Dam, and dozens of ghost towns . . .

The top state for mining silver and gold . . .

This is the Silver State—Nevada!

Did You Know?

Las Vegas is known as the "Wedding Capital of the World." Wedding ceremonies can be arranged and performed in a short time. The Little White Chapel even has a drive-up window where couples can get married in five minutes.

The theater in the Hilton Hotel in Reno has the world's largest stage. The nearly 50,000-square-foot stage can hold several thousand people.

On October 29, 1978, James Schelich placed $1 in a Las Vegas slot machine and won $275,000.

Nevada is a state of extremes. It has the country's highest marriage rate. Yet, it also has the highest divorce rate. Nevada has the country's highest rate of people who join the armed services. However, it also has the country's highest school-dropout rate. Nevada has the lowest percentage of people with health insurance. Yet, it is first in job growth.

The MGM Grand Hotel and Theme Park in Las Vegas opened in 1993 as the world's largest hotel. It has more than 5,000 rooms.

Many coins from the Carson City mint are valuable today. An 1870 Carson City twenty-dollar gold piece is now worth up to $100,000.

Jiggs, south of Elko, was named for a comic-strip character. Other Nevada towns with unusual names include Jackpot, Toy, Rabbithole, and Searchlight.

People eighteen and older can adopt wild horses and burros from Nevada. The adoption fee is $125 for a horse and $75 for a burro. People interested in adopting an animal may contact: National Wild Horse and Burro Program, Bureau of Land Management, P.O. Box 12000, Reno, Nevada 89520.

Nevada has a town called Adaven. That's *Nevada* spelled backward. A town near the border with California and Arizona is called Cal Nev Ari (for *California-Nevada-Arizona*).

The setting of the hit television show "Bonanza" was the Virginia City area.

The largest cutthroat trout ever caught was fished from Pyramid Lake in 1925. This huge fish weighed forty-one pounds.

Shirley Scheller of the Blue Diamond Center auto-truck stop near Las Vegas won the 1994 "Most Refreshing Waitress Contest." The sixty-one-year-old Scheller won over 11,000 other waitresses.

Elko was named the "Best Small Town in America" in 1993.

Nevada Information

State flag

Sagebrush

Area: 110,540 square miles (the seventh-biggest state)

Greatest Distance North to South: 478 miles

Greatest Distance East to West: 318 miles

Borders: Oregon and Idaho to the north; Utah and Arizona to the east; California to the south and west

Highest Point: Boundary Peak in western Nevada, 13,140 feet above sea level

Lowest Point: Along the Colorado River, 470 feet above sea level

Hottest Recorded Temperature: 124° F. (at Laughlin, on June 28, 1994)

Coldest Recorded Temperature: -50° F. (at San Jacinto, on January 8, 1937)

Statehood: The thirty-sixth state, on October 31, 1864

Origin of Name: In Spanish, *Nevada* means "snowfall," which refers to the state's snowcapped mountains

Capital: Carson City

Counties: 17

United States Representatives: 2

State Senators: 21

State Assembly Members: 42

State Song: "Home Means Nevada," by Bertha Raffetto

State Motto: "All for Our Country"

Nicknames: "Silver State," "Sagebrush State," "Battle Born State"

State Seal: Adopted in 1866

State Flag: Adopted in 1929

State Colors: Silver and blue

State Flower: Sagebrush

State Bird: Mountain bluebird

State Reptile: Desert tortoise

State Rock: Sandstone

State Animal: Desert bighorn sheep   **State Fossil:** Ichthyosaur

State Fish: Lahontan cutthroat trout   **State Metal:** Silver

State Grass: Indian rice grass

State Gemstones: Nevada turquoise; Virgin Valley black fire opal

State Trees: Single-leaf piñon; bristlecone pine

Some Rivers: Humboldt, Truckee, Carson, Walker, Virgin, Muddy, Colorado

Some Lakes: Tahoe, Pyramid, Mead, Walker

Some Deserts: Amaragosa, Smoke Creek, Black Rock

Some Mountain Ranges: Sierra Nevada, Shoshone, Ruby, Egan, Snake

Wildlife: Desert bighorn sheep, mustangs, wild burros, pronghorns, mule deer, coyotes, jackrabbits, porcupines, foxes, bobcats, gophers, skunks, badgers, desert tortoises, Gila monsters, chuckwallas, zebratail lizards, rattlesnakes, mountain kingsnakes, mountain bluebirds, hummingbirds, bald eagles, golden eagles, hawks, falcons, pelicans, osprey, ducks, geese, sage hens, many other birds, trout, bass, catfish, carp, cui-ui

Manufactured Products: Meat, candy, potato chips, other packaged foods, concrete, metal products, industrial machinery and equipment, computers, electrical equipment, chemicals, newspapers, other printed materials

Farm Products: Beef cattle, dairy cows, sheep, hay, grapes, onions, potatoes, barley, wheat

Mining Products: Gold, silver, diatomite, oil, sand and gravel, clay, opals, turquoise, lead, crushed stone, salt

Population: 1,201,833, thirty-ninth among the states (1990 U.S. Census Bureau figures)

Major Cities (1990 Census):

Las Vegas	258,295	Carson City	40,443
Reno	133,850	Elko	14,736
Henderson	64,942	Boulder City	12,567
Sparks	53,367	Fallon	6,438
North Las Vegas	47,707	Winnemucca	6,134

Piñon pine

Mountain bluebird

Desert tortoise

Nevada History

About 11,000 B.C.—The first people reach Nevada

About 300 B.C.—People known as Basket Makers are in Nevada

About A.D. 900—Nevada's Anasazi Indian culture is at its peak

About A.D. 1150—The Anasazi disappear from Nevada

1776—The United States is founded; Francisco Garcés, a Spanish priest, becomes the first-known European in Nevada

1821—Mexico gains its independence from Spain and claims Spain's North American lands, including Nevada

1826—Fur-trader and explorer Jedediah Smith becomes the first-known American in Nevada

1843—American John C. Frémont, guided by Kit Carson, explores northwestern Nevada

1846—The Mexican War starts between the United States and Mexico

1848—The United States wins the Mexican War; Mexico gives up Nevada and other southwestern lands to the United States; gold is found in California, prompting a rush of people through Nevada

1851—Mormons build a trading post that becomes Genoa, Nevada's first non-Indian settlement

1858—Carson City is begun; Nevada's first newspaper, the *Territorial Enterprise,* is published at Genoa

1859—The Comstock Lode is discovered; Virginia City is begun nearby

1861—The Nevada Territory is established

1861-65—About 1,100 Nevadans help the Union win the Civil War

1864—On October 31, Nevada becomes the thirty-sixth state

1870—The Carson City mint opens

1874—The University of Nevada opens in Elko

Miners in a mule car at the Comstock Lode in the 1870s

1886—The University of Nevada moves to Reno

1893—The Carson City mint ends its operations

1900—Jim Butler discovers silver at Tonopah

1902—Gold is found at Goldfield; Congress passes the Newlands Reclamation Act, which provides federal funds for irrigation

1907—Nevada's Newlands Irrigation Project, the first federal irrigation project in the nation, is completed

1917-18—About 5,000 Nevadans help the United States win World War I

1929-39—The Great Depression closes banks and hurts farming, mining, and industry nationwide

1931—Nevada legalizes gambling and makes it easy to obtain a divorce

1936—Hoover Dam is completed

1941-45—About 20,000 Nevadans and large amounts of Nevada metals help the United States win World War II

1951—Nuclear-weapons testing begins at the Nevada Test Site

1957—The University of Nevada at Las Vegas (UNLV) is founded

1962—Maude Frazier becomes Nevada's first woman lieutenant governor

1963—Nuclear explosions at the Nevada Test Site are moved underground

1964—Nevada celebrates 100 years of statehood

1980—A fire at the Las Vegas MGM Grand Hotel kills eighty-four people

1983—Barbara Vucanovich becomes the first woman to serve Nevada in the U.S. House of Representatives

1986—Great Basin National Park is established in Nevada

1990—Frankie Sue Del Papa is elected Nevada's first woman attorney general

1994—Nevada's population climbs to 1.5 million

MAP KEY

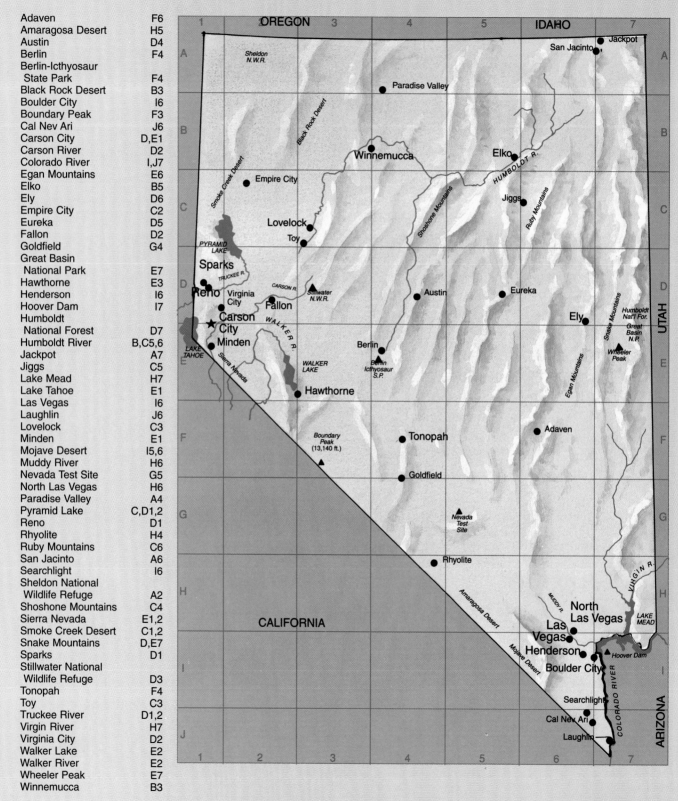

GLOSSARY

artificial: Not occurring naturally

buckaroo: A cowboy

butte: A steep hill or mountain that rises sharply above the nearby land

cactus: A plant known for its ability to live in a dry place

canyon: A deep, steep-sided valley

capital: The city that is the seat of government

capitol: The building in which the government meets

casino: A room or building used for gambling

climate: The typical weather of a region

cui-ui: An ancient sucker fish found only in Pyramid Lake

dam: A structure built on a river to hold back water

drought: A long dry spell

dust devil: A whirlwind of sand and dust that occurs over a desert

fossil: The remains of an animal or a plant that lived long ago

ghost town: A town where buildings still stand but few or no people remain

irrigation: The watering of land through dams, canals, and other artificial methods

legislature: A lawmaking body

mesa: A flat-topped mountain or hill

million: A thousand thousand (1,000,000)

mustang: A small, wild horse

pogonip: A thick winter fog containing frost crystals that occurs in mountain valleys in the western United States

population: The number of people in a place

rodeo: A contest in which cowboys and cowgirls ride horses and rope cattle

sagebrush: A desert shrub that covers one-fifth of Nevada and is Nevada's state flower

territory: The name for a part of the United States before it becomes a state

wildlife refuge: A place where animals are protected

Sand Mountain, near Fallon

PICTURE ACKNOWLEDGMENTS

INDEX

Page numbers in boldface type indicate illustrations.

ABOUT THE AUTHORS

Dennis and Judith Fradin have coauthored several books in the From Sea to Shining Sea series. The Fradins both graduated from Northwestern University in 1967. Dennis has been a professional writer for twenty years, and has published 150 books. His works for Childrens Press include the Young People's Stories of Our States series, the Disaster! series, and the Thirteen Colonies series. Judith earned her M.A. in literature from Northwestern University and taught high-school and college English for many years. The Fradins, who are the parents of Anthony, Diana, and Michael, live in Evanston, Illinois.